The Reinvention Of Gyms

A step-by-step guide on why you need coaching and community, not just a gym membership.

Originally released in the United Kingdom by Josh Ware in 2024.

ISBN: 978-1-3999-9100-1

This book does not offer personalised health and fitness advice. Rather, it aims to provide a general overview of our one-on-one client interactions. The author explicitly disclaims any liability, loss, or risk incurred directly or indirectly from the use or application of any content within this work.

Printed and bound in Great Britain by:
Book Printing UK Remus House, Coltsfoot Drive, Woodston, Peterborough PE2 9BF

I dedicate this book to every gym-goer that has been let down by the traditional gym model.

If you have joined a gym hoping to reach your fitness goals and failed, then this book is for you.

I hope the ideas in this book assist you in taking total control of your health and fitness once and for all.

Committed to your success,

Josh

Contents

1. Setting The Scene

Having had over 16 years' experience in the industry and owning my own gym for the past 6 years, I have had the privilege of transforming hundreds of lives. I believe the traditional gym membership model is flawed, and that it is my personal responsibility to change that.

Joining the gym and embracing health and fitness literally changed my life. Without taking charge of my own health and fitness, I wouldn't be where I am today.

In this book, I'll explore why most people with gym memberships fail to reach their goals and why the traditional gym model is outdated and ineffective.

My mission is to change this, one gym and coaching facility at a time.

2. Normal Gym Memberships Don't Work

It is a stark reality that the majority of individuals struggle to achieve their health and fitness goals with a standard gym membership. The old and outdated gym membership model is broken. But before delving into the power of community and coaching methodologies in fitness, we need to understand what a typical gym membership experience entails and why it often falls short in nearly all circumstances. Let's examine a typical gym membership experience.

You begin your journey by doing a search online or by responding to an advertisement about joining a gym. You look on their website at all of the shiny gym equipment, perhaps noticing that they have a pool, and confirm the availability of classes. After a quick search on their social media or website, you can proceed to sign up online or request a callback from a member of their team. At this juncture, you have either enrolled or engaged in a conversation with one of the team members regarding the facilities. If you are fortunate, they will ask what you are looking for and enquire about your fitness goals. You are then guided through the pricing options, with the choice to either waiver the induction, or schedule one in with a level 2 gym instructor or level 3 personal trainer. Upon booking your induction and possibly a few classes, you're eager to embark on your journey towards a fitter and healthier you.

When the day of your induction arrives, you feel apprehensive – understandably so. You're uncertain of what to expect, who you are going to meet, and the environment you are about to enter. You arrive, receive a generic overview of gym equipment and how to use them, and you are handed a standardised routine. After this session, you're left to navigate the gym floor alone, surrounded by seasoned gym-goers. This experience can be intimidating, and in some cases this discomfort might lead you to favour attending classes instead, forgoing the gym floor all together. Each class has an instructor leading the session and provides guidance in a group setting, accompanied by energetic music. This perhaps makes you feel more at ease, and so you schedule group exercise sessions, enticed by their descriptions and the promise of calorie burning, fat torching and strength building. This sounds like you have found the solution you have been looking for!

However, this is not the case. The class instructor doesn't know who you are, they don't know your fitness levels, they don't know about any medical conditions that you may or may not have, they don't know what exercises you can do safely nor how mobile you are, or if you even have the confidence to try any of the exercises for the first time in front of a group of strangers that you have only just met. Alongside this, the brightly lit room you are in with big open windows showcases the class' popularity to all potential new members, and so you feel watched and uncomfortable. The instructor then takes you through the 45-60 minute session and because the instructor doesn't know what you are capable of or your goals, they take you through a generic workout that is suitable for everyone, lacking personalisation or progression.

This routine continues for around 4 weeks and in my experience, I have witnessed most members are attending less than twice per week by the end of the first month of joining. Dissatisfied with the lack of results, you speak to one of the receptionists, who suggests that you consider personal training for tailored guidance.

Finally, you believe that you have discovered your solution. You have tried doing it your way, but that didn't work, so having a personal trainer is the next best option! Alas, however, that comes with an additional cost. Personal training sessions, ideally conducted three times per week, range anywhere from £35 per hour to £100+. If we were to work on the lower end of the scale at £35ph, three times a week equates to £454 each month! I don't know about you, but I don't know many people who could afford that monthly outgoing regularly. If you live in a metropolitan city, you could easily be paying double or even triple that amount.

This gives you a brief synopsis on why the majority of gym members are set up for disappointment from the outset and rarely reach their goals. The traditional gym membership model sets you up for failure; it isn't set up around member success or achieving results. It is more about getting people through the door and adopting a high-volume approach.

There are various points of failure within this model that hinders your progress towards your health and fitness goals, such as at your initial interaction where you engage in a generic conversation outlining the facility's appealing features but they end up knowing nothing about you or what you would like to achieve. You sign up, pay your fees and start booking sessions. Despite this, ultimately, the novelty wears off, and you become a 'sleeper member'.

When I first started in the industry, 'sleeper members' were frequently discussed, alongside strategies to expand this membership base. A sleeper member is an individual who pays for a gym membership but rarely, if ever, attends – the ideal member most gyms try to cultivate.

I have participated in meetings and masterminds solely focused on enhancing these statistics. The key is to charge a fee that safeguards the gym's profit margins yet is not high enough that members notice the monthly deduction from their bank accounts. Let's face it, how often do you review your bank statements for direct debits? Even if you do notice the deductions, you probably don't think about cancelling straight away, because having a gym membership is good for you, right? Perhaps it might even give you a kick to get back into going to the gym, maybe you think 'I'll start again next week?'.

From my experience and what I have witnessed in my gym is that the majority of gym members cease attending in the first 30 days and continue to pay for at least 6 months before cancelling. By then, you have reverted back to square one, or in most cases, you are in a worse off position to where you began.

You have been set up for failure before you even start, and this scenario plays out in gyms up and down the country, time and time again. I think it's quite evident who the winner is here.

An Alternative – The Coached Experience

Imagine you are searching online or responding to an advertisement about joining a gym. The idea of working with a gym that offers coaching appeals to you, although you're not entirely sure what it entails. You go ahead and schedule a 'discovery call' with a member of the coaching team via a link on their website, who are experienced in helping clients just like you.

The call comes and after polite introductions, the coach informs you that they only work with clients that they are certain they can help. Their approach is emphasised as prescriptive, with solutions tailored to your individual needs, allowing your specific goals to be met. This is done in a manner which can be described as a friendly interrogation, but be reassured that by the end of the call you will be offered a place on the coaching program provided you are a good fit. This is achieved by using a decision framework and the coach genuinely believing that they can help you. If it is deemed that actually the program may not be right for you, you may be signposted to another suitable professional or facility.

It is already apparent the difference between merely taking your money and leaving you to figure the gym out for yourself versus a facility and support network focused solely on you, your goals and ensuring that you achieve them. We will go into further details about the discovery call once I have told you more about me and my 'why'.

3. Who Am I?

Now that you have some insight into why the traditional gym membership model is flawed, allow me to properly introduce myself and explain why I have authority in this field.

I'm Josh, the owner and lead coach at Future Bodies Gym, based in Devon. I am on a mission to revolutionise the outdated, ineffective membership model that is so prevalent in gyms. I'm breaking down the barriers of tradition and establishing a fitness revolution, where everyone can thrive and achieve their goals.

I find it incredibly disheartening that most gym members never reach their health and fitness goals and end up paying for an unused gym membership. I find this unacceptable and feel morally obligated to change this. I am determined to shake up the old, ineffective model and bring in the new.

My passion for health and fitness runs deep, as joining the gym quite literally changed my life. To understand more about me, it's important to trace it back to where it all began. I was born in Exeter and spent much of my childhood in Crediton, where I attended primary school. My parents separated when I was 2, and my dad met my step-mum when I was 3. I have fond memories of growing up in Crediton and Exeter until I turned 11.

My time in primary school was great, I was blessed to have a good group of friends and good home life and there really isn't anything noteworthy to say other than I had a typical happy upbringing with parents who were separated.

During my early years, I was always skinny and wore glasses. I had to wear an eyepatch due to having a lazy eye, and I had to undergo an operation to correct it. Despite these challenges, I never experienced bullying or teasing.

After some time, my mum moved us to Exeter, and I changed primary schools. It was quite a shock to transition to a new school where many had already formed friendships. I vividly recall wandering around during lunchtime, feeling lost and unsure of whom to approach. Then, one of the teachers introduced me to a boy called Chris. It was his first day at the school as well, and he seemed just as bewildered and out of place. Thus began a friendship that has lasted decades, culminating in me delivering a best man's speech at his wedding.

When the time came to start thinking about secondary schools the topic of moving in with my dad was raised. To cut to the chase I chose to move in with my dad, who lived in North Tawton at the time. There wasn't a specific reason for the move, it just happened, but it was a significant change for me and suddenly, I found myself craving more attention and security, feeling incredibly alone.

My mum had always provided warmth and maternal love,

and I soon realised how much I missed it. Reflecting on this, I now see how challenging it was for a young boy to cope with such a transition. Little did I know the psychological impact it would have and the challenges I would face in the coming months and years.

It took me a while to adjust to my new life, with its new routines, another new school, my newly altered full-time relationships with my dad and step-mum and a less hands-on relationship with my biological mum. It wasn't until I was in school that I realised how unique my situation was. Everyone I spoke to either had parents who were still together, or if they had separated, they primarily stayed with their mother.

This was also the start of when I began to experience psychological trauma. I want to shield my children from certain aspects of my past, so I am not going to delve into what this entailed, however, it affected me greatly. So much so, this experience manifested itself into a verbal stammer. This caused difficulty in communicating clearly, low self-confidence and a profound insecurity.

For those unfamiliar with stammering, stammering is a communication impairment characterised by disruptions and stoppages in the fluency and timing of speech. It affects approximately one percent of adults and four percent of children. Although it was difficult, this stage of my life is an integral part of my story and plays a vital part in why I am where I am today.

My secondary school years weren't adorned with epic tales or extraordinary events. I sort of drifted through school without firmly fitting into any particular group or stereotype. It felt like being a puzzle piece without a matching spot in the grand teenage social mosaic. By this point, my stammer and low self-confidence had been a lingering presence for years, and it escalated when I reached sixth form. I gradually found myself drifting away from many of my closest friends. Why? Because I didn't quite align with the mould that they had in mind.

It all started with something seemingly insignificant – not receiving an invite for a lunchtime car ride. We were all excited about passing our driving tests and we didn't need much reason to hit the road. But on that day, the invitation never arrived, and my main circle of friends departed without me. As time wore on, my messages went unanswered and before I knew it, I found myself isolated with no one to turn to.

This phase of my life served as a stark reminder that sometimes even those you expect to stand by you can suddenly turn away. It was a lonely journey of self-discovery, but it also marked the beginning of something greater, something for which I am now truly grateful.

I had always been somewhat unconventional, thinking and acting in ways that set me apart from my peers, steadfastly refusing to conform to the status quo. I have always wanted to be part of something bigger – even though I didn't really know what that was or what that would look like.

When my friendship groups dissipated, my mental health took a hit and my confidence began to crumble further. Then, my stammer became an unexpected hurdle that began to hinder me in ways I had never anticipated.

I have had to undergo extensive therapy to unravel the complexities of my stammer. Childhood experiences and the rejection of my closest friendship group definitely played a part in its development.

This caused a cycle of negative self-talk, convincing myself that I was never going to be good enough. My self-perception became so negative that I viewed myself as unworthy, which further fuelled the development of my stammer. I became increasingly fearful of judgement with every word I uttered, eventually losing the confidence to even ask questions.

There are two types of stammer - an overt stammer and a covert stammer.

An overt stammer is one you may have encountered before, where the person attempts to say a word but gets stuck on certain syllables. For example, "I went r-r-r-round the r-r-r-roundabout" or "H-h-h-how are you?" Sometimes, a person might get stuck on a word or syllable for numerous attempts, sometimes as many as 20 or more.

A covert stammerer, on the other hand, will switch words at the last minute if they feel a block coming on. However, this tactic has limitations, and their choice of words can become severely restricted. If a negative experience is associated with a particular word, the individual may find themselves stuttering on that word in future instances.

I concealed my stammer remarkably well. I felt deeply ashamed of it, and even when I brought it to my parents' attention, they couldn't understand what I was talking about because I never stammered in front of them at home. From my experience, my stammer was highly situational. I could freely converse and ask questions at home with my mum, whereas in the outside world I suddenly struggled to communicate in the way I desired.

One of the lowest points in my life occurred while I was working as a waiter. Despite my stammer, I was determined to not let it hold me back. However, on that particular day, as I approached a table I stumbled over my words. I couldn't even introduce myself, say my own name or ask simple questions. Leaving that table, tears welled up in my eyes. I felt utterly inadequate, worthless and my self-confidence hit rock bottom.

Another difficult moment happened during a family Christmas gathering. As we passed around gifts, I found myself unable to express gratitude for a present, sitting there mute, unable to voice my thoughts and opinions. I vividly recall breaking down in tears in the car with my mum afterward. My stammer had tightened its grip, worsening and severely impacting my relationships with those closest to me. However, what I failed to realise at the time was that this seemingly insurmountable challenge would ultimately set me on the path to where I find myself today.

It is important to note that I have undergone a significant amount of therapy, which has provided me with profound insights into my past and helped me understand why I am the way I am. Counselling helped me to unravel the intricate knots tying me to my stammer. It was my way of peeling back the layers, understanding the complex tapestry of experiences and emotions that influenced my stammer and confidence.

Through therapy, I made a conscious decision to overcome my challenges. Reflecting on my journey and the therapy I've received, I now appreciate it all. It has shaped me into the person I am today and positioned me where I am now. I realise that if my experiences had been different, I might not be where I am today.

Today, I have a wonderful family, a beautiful home, a nice car, I'm healthy, fit and strong, and have a thriving business that provides for my family's needs. I wouldn't trade my past for anything because it has brought me to this point.

Before delving further into this book, I want to emphasize the importance of seeking therapy if you're dealing with unresolved issues. Therapy still carries a stigma, but it's time to move past it. If something is holding you back, address it and seek help.

Even now, I continue to work with a performance coach who helps me optimise my decision making. I also journal, which helps me to release mental pressure when life becomes overwhelming.

Our past experiences shape us into unique individuals, each with our own strengths and weaknesses. Rather than viewing our past as a limitation, we should see it as a source of strength. When we embrace our uniqueness and leverage from our past experiences, we unlock unparalleled potential for growth and success.

The reason I'm dedicated to what I do now is to transform lives and unlock true potential, both physically and mentally for every client I come into contact with. Thanks to taking charge of my mental and physical well-being, I've achieved things that the younger version of myself never thought possible.

I refuse to accept anyone telling me I'm not good enough or unworthy. This inner drive to defy the odds and carve out my own path in life is my superpower, and it's within all of us. Our life experiences fuel this power. You're always in control of your destiny. Sometimes you just need that wake-up call to take action. Perhaps reading this book could be that very wake-up call you've been waiting for.

4. The Start of My Career in Health and Fitness

My adventure began with a simple desire to bolster my confidence and gain control over my stammer. I had come across numerous articles linking stammering to social anxiety and self-confidence issues, prompting me to join the gym. As previously mentioned, I was slender, and deep down, I was uncomfortable with my appearance.

At that juncture in my life, self-doubt was a constant companion and to combat it I embarked on a journey of self-improvement and confidence-building. The gym wasn't just a place for me to improve my physical fitness – it became my sanctuary. There, I not only honed my body but also fortified my inner resolve and discovered my true self. It was where I felt in command of my emotions, actions and self-worth.

I devoured every article on weightlifting, various training regimens, tempo-based weight training, muscle gain and fat loss strategies. I immersed myself in every detail about working out and transforming my physique. I was consumed by my passion. In a sense, the gym sculpted my physique, while counselling chiselled away at my emotional barriers linked to my stammer.

This phase of my journey marked a turning point, where

my physical strength and emotional resilience intersected, thus shaping the person I was becoming. In this unfolding narrative, I discovered the exhilarating sensation of seizing control and truly owning my path.

In pursuit of purpose and fuelled by my passion for fitness, I ventured into the world of competitive bodybuilding. It was a solitary pursuit that suited me perfectly, requiring not only rigorous training but also unwavering dedication to a strict diet and calorie restriction. To turn this aspiration into reality, I made the choice to drop out of my A-levels halfway through my first year and transitioned to working full-time as a waiter, saving up money while I pursued my newfound ambition in competitive bodybuilding.

For a year, I delved deep into the realm of competitive bodybuilding, uncovering an unquenchable love for training and pushing my limits. This newfound passion ignited a profound desire within me.

Experiencing firsthand the transformative power of taking control of your health and fitness and dedicating yourself to becoming the best version of you possible, I soon found colleagues seeking my training advice. I began offering to work out with them, guiding them on their fitness journey. It was during this time that the idea of pursuing a career in health and fitness crystallised in my mind.

Moreover, I aspired to do a job I loved, so I chose to become a personal trainer to share the life-changing impact of fitness with others. I then embarked on researching the optimal pathway to achieving this goal.

During my research, I came across a six-week intensive personal training course in Spain. Excitedly, I shared my aspirations with my parents and two months later, I found myself boarding a plane, ready to chase my dreams.

My time in there proved to be nothing short of extraordinary. It presented me with an opportunity to reinvent myself and take control of my narrative, free from the biases of my past. I forged lasting friendships, some of which stand as cherished parts of my life today. Most importantly, it strengthened my resolve to pursue a career centred on helping others achieve their fitness goals and bolster their emotional resilience.

Spain wasn't just a destination, it was a transformative chapter in my journey. There, I honed my skills, cultivated lifelong connections and reaffirmed my unwavering commitment to this path. It marked a pivotal moment that set me on course to realise my passion for guiding others toward their best selves through fitness.

As my intensive training course drew to a close, I recognised the need to have a well-defined game plan. Enamoured with the Spanish lifestyle, my love for training and the enjoyment of coaching others, I started looking for personal trainer positions, particularly focusing on fitness retreats and boot camps in sunny Spain.

You might be curious if I succeeded in finding someone daring enough to hire a freshly certified personal trainer, someone willing to help me live out my dream of working abroad while doing a job I was convinced I'd adore. Well, guess what? I did! It felt as though the stars had aligned to grant me this opportunity, and I couldn't have been more excited about the journey ahead.

I spent eight fulfilling months working in Spain. During this time, with two and a half years of training behind me and a continued investment in self-improvement through counselling and mentorship, I made the decision to pursue my first bodybuilding show. It was a daunting undertaking, but I was determined to push my boundaries to the next level.

To my surprise, I excelled. At just nineteen years old, with only two and a half years of training under my belt, I earned a coveted spot in the prestigious European Qualifiers. Out of the whole of England, only twenty-one of us were selected. Whilst it was an incredible achievement, it soon became apparent that this wasn't my true calling.

When I first immersed myself in the world of bodybuilding I couldn't help but admire the dedication and remarkable physiques of those involved. They seemed to embody the epitome of fitness, strength and health. However, as I ventured deeper into this world, I soon realised that their approach was far from sustainable. The immense sacrifices they made, especially in terms of their social lives, were monumental. Moreover, the extreme dieting and drastic weight fluctuations they underwent appeared detrimental to overall well-being. And don't even get me started on the consuming obsession with food; it hardly fostered genuine body confidence or optimal performance.

In fact, and I maintain this viewpoint steadfastly today, I strongly disagree with bodybuilding as a holistic approach. My vision was, and still is, crystal clear: I aimed to embody fitness, strength and health while nurturing an unwavering sense of confidence to tackle life's challenges head-on. I learnt, however, that bodybuilding only partially aligned with these aspirations. This realisation marked a pivotal moment in my journey, igniting a quest for a more comprehensive and fulfilling path to personal well-being. Throughout my bodybuilding journey, a profound philosophy took root within me – one centred on self-improvement, resilience and the pursuit of genuine passion to become the best version of oneself.

Here's the beauty of life, however – it has a way of guiding us back to our origins. As time passed, I found myself yearning for the familiarity of home and began exploring options to return. Little did I know, a remarkable opportunity was about to unfold.

In my hometown, a new gym was preparing to open its doors and they were actively seeking personal trainers.

Fuelled by curiosity and brimming with enthusiasm, I reached out and had a conversation with the owners. To my surprise and delight, they offered me the job on the spot!

With excitement coursing through me, I packed my bags and headed home, ready to embrace my new role. Unbeknownst to me, this gym would serve as a milestone in my journey. It was here that I further honed my skills and further explored my potential as a fitness professional. I poured every ounce of my being into the job, often working from dawn till dusk to accommodate as many clients as possible.

After just 8 months, my efforts bore fruit and I was promoted to Assistant Manager. It was an opportunity to contribute to the growth and direction of the business, and I embraced it with the same unwavering commitment that had always defined my work ethic.

However, amidst the progression, a realization dawned on me: I didn't like answering to a boss or not being fully in control of my career. I wanted to be in charge of my own path and live life on my own terms, while doing something I loved. I just didn't know what my next steps should be.

When I found myself in a small gym with limited growth prospects, my thirst for knowledge and personal development remained unquenched. I aspired to create a thriving business that would allow me to pursue my passion for changing lives.

So, I decided to pursue higher education in order to earn a degree in business, ensuring that when I was ready to take the leap, I would understand the mechanics of running a business and be able to pull it off. To do this, I needed to complete a year-long course to qualify for university, having left my A-Levels incomplete. I resigned from my job as an employed Personal Trainer and Assistant Manager, transitioning to freelance work and continuing to rent space at the very gym where I once helped manage. Twelve months later, I emerged from college with the equivalent of three A-Levels. I then enrolled in a fast-track 2-year Business Management program at university.

Balancing the demands of academia with running my freelance personal training business, I poured my everything into both endeavours. After two years and while still maintaining full-time work hours, I proudly graduated with a first-class honours degree. Throughout this journey, one thing remained constant – my unwavering love for exercise and its profound impact on my physical and mental well-being.

Upon graduation, I found myself in need of immediate financial stability. I embarked on a relentless job hunt, applying for every graduate manager position available. My plan was to continue personal training clients on weekends whilst working in a graduate management role with a good salary. This would allow me to save diligently, eventually realising my dream of starting my own gym and coaching business.

The truth be told, finding a graduate job that interested and inspired me was next to impossible. I applied for many roles, but unbeknownst to me before you even go to interview there are a series of numerical and theoretical tests you have to pass. This is designed so that big industries and employers can screen out anybody who does not have a certain IQ. I do not profess to be hyper intelligent, however, I had just achieved a first class honours and was hopeful that my chances of securing a graduate job were high. I was also able to hold my own in conversation and bring reason to the table if I got to the interview stage. But it never got to that stage for me - I am not ashamed to say that I failed every single test posed to me over the course of three months. We all have certain skill sets in life, and passing these tests was going to take me a very, very long time.

My accommodation at university was coming to an end and I had to either move back in with my parents or find somewhere else to live, but that was proving difficult considering I couldn't find a graduate role!

An advert was released for a graduate recruitment consultant in London, to which I had no idea what it was, but thought that it sounded different and it offered a promising salary. I applied, and to my surprise, I was invited to an interview in London. The interview went well and I was successful in being offered the job. For anyone who's not sure on what a recruitment consultant does, in simple terms you head hunt corporate roles and fill those roles for companies. My role was to find facilities' managers within the M25, earning a percentage commission based on the salary of the role.

The role was based in the centre of London and at the very least it would enable me to be in the city with plenty of opportunity to find my feet and get established. To say I had no idea what I was walking into was an understatement.

There I was, a lad from Devon, trying to find his way in the big city. I remember heading up to London a couple of weeks before I was due to move up there to look at properties to rent. I looked at a small 2 bedroomed flat, thinking that the £1,000 in rent each month was ludicrously expensive. What I didn't realise was that the listing was actually £1,000 per week! The realisation soon dawned on me that I was going to need every bit of my income and sales commission to actually be able to survive in the city.

And so, I found a place to live in social housing. It was in an area of North London called Wood Green, and it cost £700 a month. This obviously meant that it came with its drawbacks, in fact, an abundance of drawbacks. These being having a single room with a small bathroom, no lounge access and having a shared kitchen with 12 other occupants. To top it off, my room was on the ground floor next to a karaoke bar! Looking back on this time, it is quite laughable really, but at the time this was the start of a spiral I didn't see coming.

I left Devon for London with high hopes of using this role as a stepping stone to move on, but this is when reality smacked me in the face. The contract I signed stated that I would be working 9-5, and so I thought that I would have ample time to study for the IQ tests and also explore other opportunities to bolster my income. This is where I soon realised that the contract wasn't worth the paper it was written on and whilst my contract may have said one thing, the reality was very different. It was made clear that we were fully expected to be at our desks by 8am and to stay well past 6pm. On top of this we had dial out targets, with all of our call times being recorded, alongside aggressive sales targets to meet from the get-go. I am happy with pressure, but this type of pressure was insane. Colleagues in the office were regularly taking illegal substances to keep themselves going and I couldn't believe that life had led me to this point.

Despite the gruelling hours, I continued to get to the gym at 6am every morning, as yet again it was my sanctuary and the only place I could go to find relief. Other than this early morning workout, I found that I had zero time to do anything else, with an hour commute each way on the jam-packed tube and commuting back to Devon each Friday to deliver over 20 hours of personal training over the weekend, just to try and keep my head above water.

It was a stage in life where within 3 months my mental health was in pieces. I had never felt more trapped, afraid and skint in my entire life! It would appear the earning potential and work life balance I was hoping for was not inline with what I had been told at interview. I was frequently calling my mum back at home and I distinctly remember having to go for a walk to talk to her due to the volume of the karaoke that was occurring just next door.

I was lost, scared and alone and I thought that I had royally screwed my life up. I felt that I had nowhere to turn to, and my self-confidence was on the floor.

It turned out that recruitment consultancy really wasn't for me. I got home from work one day to yet another karaoke night about to start and I snapped. I phoned my mum and told her that I was going home – I was done and needed to reevaluate my life. The very next day, I packed my suitcase, hopped on a train and sent my resignation letter to my boss whilst en route home. As every mile passed, I felt the tightness of anxiety leave my chest.

When I got home, I had a deep sense of shame and failure. I thought that after all of the work that I had put in, I would finally be getting somewhere. But no, I was back where it all started, living back with my mum as a 22-year-old man and no real way of realising my ambition.

I had a week off to recuperate and try to collect my thoughts and then I started back on the job hunt. I picked up a few extra hours of personal training, and it was there that one conversation led me to a remarkable opportunity. It was with one of my very first clients whose husband was a successful businessman. He had recently taken over a struggling family business and was searching for a graduate manager to mentor and eventually run the company. That is where I stepped in.

We met and he offered me the job on our first meeting. Starting as a Graduate Manager – I had finally got the break I was searching for! I threw myself into the role and gave that company everything I had, all while continuing to work with my clients on weekends. Working side by side with my mentor, I poured my heart and soul into the job. Two years flew by and together we transformed the business from a £600K per year operation, to one generating over £1.8M in revenue. Along the way, I received well-deserved pay raises, managed to buy my first house, and built up surplus savings.

It was then I started actively planning how to set up my own business and put the wheels in motion to make it a reality. I started to explore local opportunities, and I heard a rumour on the grapevine that my old gym was up for sale. It was in dire straits, but I saw it as an opportunity to take total control of my destiny.

Without hesitation, I sealed the deal with a simple handshake. And just like that, Future Bodies Gym was reborn under my ownership. It marked the beginning of a new chapter, a chance to make a lasting impact on the lives of those who walked through its doors, and a way for me to fulfil a passion that had been my constant companion since the age of 16.

5. The Beginning of Future Bodies

Future Bodies was in dire straits with serious losses on the books, but I knew I could develop something special. I will be the first to admit, however, that I didn't really have a plan other than to work as hard as I could and build the Future Bodies' name.

When I first started, there were minimal classes and none of the 4-person team delivered any personal training. I quickly developed a process to sell personal training sessions alongside gym memberships, and my own personal diary filled up quickly, and soon enough I was working 16-hour days. The rest of the team's diaries filled up too, and I even had some external self-employed personal trainers' working for me.

Additionally, I began to offer generic fitness classes. Before I knew it, 18 months had gone by and the ship was finally stabilised. The losses had stopped, and we had started to break even. Members were happy with their experience and our name was really starting to get around town.

The downside to this was I was working every hour given to me. I had almost stopped training myself, I barely spent any time with friends or family and all of my time was focused on Future Bodies.

In order to purchase the gym, I had to take out some

big loans and I could not default on them. This is a period of my life I remember well – I was constantly in a state of fight or flight, stressed and not sleeping well. I couldn't sit still. I constantly had to be doing something, and the list of things I had to get done was endlessly getting longer. Of course, there was going to be a breaking point.

I became unwell. I was tired all the time, so much so I couldn't keep my eyes open when not in the throes of work and personal training. I am also asthmatic, which is primarily worse when the seasons are changing, which of course they were at this particular time. My asthma was uncontrollable, I had no energy and every time I coughed I had excruciating pain shoot through my head and down my neck. I couldn't warm up, I wasn't eating or drinking and I was trembling from overuse of my inhalers.

Jess, my partner, is a paramedic, and although she had been telling me for weeks to rest and speak to my GP or asthma nurse, I didn't listen to her. This was until I was absolutely on my knees, and I finally gave in. She frogmarched me into the car and she took me to the emergency department where I was promptly admitted and hooked up to monitors and drips.

I slept properly for what felt like the first time in weeks, but was raring to be discharged and get back to work. I asked the doctor if I could go home, to which he replied and said that he had never seen a 25-year-old patient who had subjected his mental and physical health to such levels of stress, and quite bluntly said unless I was discharging myself I would not be going home that day. He gave me a stern talking to and advised me that I needed to recover before even thinking about returning to work.

This issue with this was for every day off work, I wasn't earning. With the loans, I literally couldn't afford to have time off. As my gym grew, so did the overheads. As soon as I was discharged, I was back to work the next day.

I knew that I wanted to provide an incredible service to my members, but it was tough finding a balance between growing the gym, managing my stress levels, trying to keep everyone happy and actually get to a point where I had a financial advantage to be able to buy my time back and bring in more staff. I came up with the idea to try and increase the membership base – more members equals more income, which would then give me the funds to pay more wages. To do this, I took on an extension of the gym.

The extension expanded the gym by 30%, and we built a new studio for classes and a revolutionary cycle studio, something the town had never seen before. We also opened a crèche, to help all of the parents who wanted to join or use us more but couldn't because of childcare.

The cycle room was kitted out by the very best lighting designer I could find, and he created a lighting experience that immersed our clients in a different reality. It was amazing! However, this was a huge project and it cost money that I didn't have. I took out more loans, maxed every credit card I had and also managed to sweet talk suppliers to extend our payment terms with them. My father-in-law took on the build, and my dad finished the work off by decorating. It really was a family affair!

This marked the start of a marketing plan that the town had never seen before. We went big, and we got our name everywhere. I sent out flyers to 13,000 homes in the local area, I spoke to the local press who released an article on us, I hired a billboard in town and did referral campaigns. The website was updated, and I also brought in a marketing agency to help who put digital eyes on my vision.

I did a two-week membership drive, utilising all marketing strategies I could. The logic was if I threw enough strategies at the wall, some of it would stick.

Within two days, our website crashed due to the volume of visitors. Our phones were off the hook and we were inundated with messages. In just one week, I had signed up over 100 members and my diary was filled with enquiries for the next four weeks.

I opened the extension proudly at the end of January 2020. The classes were all fully booked with waiting lists. The gym was pumping, the atmosphere electric. It was amazing. I thought I had finally done it, and that I had created a gym that I had dreamt of. I even had to speak to a neighbouring landowner to rent a small piece of his land so I could build our own Future Bodies' car park as there just weren't enough parking spaces to fulfil demand without more space.

Typically, things don't go to plan, but this curveball, I, and the rest of the world, did not see coming. Everything came to a halt.

6. Curveball

There was this rumour circulating globally of a flu that was making people poorly. The news was limited, but it had something to do with China and that it was starting to worry people. Things started to get hard to buy, and prices started to go up. The news then came of the first confirmed case of coronavirus in the UK. I felt uneasy, but confident it wouldn't affect us down in the southwest, so carried on as normal. But of course, things escalated, and cases began to rise, and they began to get closer to home. News circulated about the possibility of a national lockdown, and this was something that I really couldn't afford to happen. I had thrown everything I had at the gym and was finally beginning to see the fruits of my labour, but I had no funds in the bank to sustain being locked down for a month, let alone longer.

I had a backup plan to take Future Bodies online if I had to, but I hadn't had the time to put a huge amount of thought into it as the gym was booming and we were barely able to keep up with demand. The thought of the entire country going into a lockdown just didn't seem feasible to me.

Myself, Jess and a few friends had planned a weekend away in St Ives and my diary was deactivated for the first time in a long time. It was lovely to get away and try to unwind after the whirlwind first few weeks of a successful expansion campaign, until we saw on the news that Boris Johnson was set to release details of a national lockdown later that day. I can honestly say the fear in my stomach was nearly enough to make me vomit. I sat with Jess and waited for what could very well be an announcement that would put me out of business.

Boris came on the television and said the words that I did not want to hear – he was locking us all down the next day. I didn't quite know what to do, so I sat in my car and uploaded a Facebook video to our members saying not to panic, we will take Future Bodies online and continue to deliver a service. Within 3 days, 250 members had cancelled their memberships.

The week that followed consisted of phoning the banks and discussing at length if there was any way that I could survive this by extending payments. I had over £75,000 in short-term loans and credit cards, which was over £4,000 per month of personal liabilities that I had to satisfy. Losing these memberships made these bills unaffordable, and that is without my own mortgage and living costs.

Of course, I wasn't alone in the worry of money during these uncertain times. The news broke that we could get various payment holidays, mortgage holidays and the business interruption loan. This, combined with the minimal reserves I had coming in from direct debit memberships meant that I had approximately 4 months of cash flow, which would ensure I would be able to pay my staff (this was prior to the furlough scheme announcement). Membership cancellations and direct debit claim backs were coming in by the dozen load each day, and everything I had worked so hard for was slipping between my fingers.

We took Future Bodies online, and we were running virtual classes 8 hours a day. We also ran virtual fitness challenges, Zoom socials and weekend outdoor meetups (when allowed). No matter how hard we tried, we were getting nowhere. We were losing memberships every day and those attending the classes didn't even cover the instructors' wages to run them. This circumstance led me on a path of self-reflection.

I had initially followed a traditional gym membership model simply because it was the norm, and I got carried away with exciting, shiny new ideas. I realised that I had never properly sat down and considered what my clients actually needed to achieve through a gym membership. So, I re-evaluated the very business I had built. Honestly, I wasn't achieving any meaningful results with my members; I wasn't impacting any lives. I had been working in a state of constant overdrive and worry for many months. It became clear that there had to be a better way.

I asked myself what I wanted to be known for and what would make me excited to go to work every day. The answer was simple - I wanted my members to achieve life-changing results. So, with that in mind, I set out to completely redesign my gym and product offering, helping clients to achieve their health and fitness goals once and for all.

However, I was stuck because I didn't really know how to convey my message or how to completely redesign my business from the ground up. So, in the final months of lockdown, I began working with a business mentor whose philosophy was to build a coaching business based on the impact you can have on a client's life. His approach resonated with me deeply. I knew I wanted to make a massive impact on my members' lives, but I wasn't sure how to achieve it. Consequently, I took one more risk and maxed out my last credit card to work with him for 12 months.

7. The Development of the #GameChangers Program

I started my first ever coached program in June 2021. This program was going to change the game when it came to getting results for my members, and hence the name #GameChangers was born. I was confident that this program was going to upend the traditional gym membership model, and the program was designed to have a massive impact on my clients' lives, enabling them to take total control of their health and fitness once and for all.

In retrospect now, the program was clunky. It was nowhere near where we are today, but it was already 10 times better than a normal gym membership. In fact, we still have a few of my first ever sign ups on the program today. They are lovingly referred to as the OGs (the originals!).

I tried to run both parts of the gym concurrently, but this was problematic. My existing and loyal members didn't understand why I was charging more for our coaching services, because we had essentially given a version of it to them for free whilst in lockdown. They couldn't understand why I was taking away some classes and replacing them with #GameChangers coached sessions. I was trying so hard to appease everyone and failing on both sides, and I was constantly trying to keep all the plates spinning, but before I knew it I was back working 16 hours a day to try and keep on top of everything.

A divide had been created in the gym between normal members and coaching clients. I received heavy criticism, being told that I was choosing to work with only the elite or those who had money, and that I had clearly forgotten that loyal members had supported me throughout lockdowns. This couldn't have been further from the truth. Yes, there was a premium charge for our fully coached services but it was an impossibility to run the #GameChangers program for a normal membership cost.

Members started to leave because they were unhappy that classes had been taken away, and I also began to lose coaching clients because they too were unhappy that they could not book in to sessions that they wanted. I had hit a ceiling. I was back to working insanely long days, there was a WhatsApp group set up by disgruntled members just to defame my character and this all took its toll.

This led to me having my first ever panic attack. I was exhausted and had constant waves of sheer panic and terror running through me, frequently thinking that I was going to be sick. I was back to not sleeping, nor was I eating. I was told by those around me constantly that I looked tired and unhealthy. I had stopped working out, would often be falling asleep in the afternoons and if I had any spare time, all I would want to do was sit in front of the television and shut the world out.

The gym had stalled, and I was in no man's land. The program wasn't established enough and the membership base was stagnant. If I were to put any more emphasis on one part of the gym, the other would directly suffer and I was stood in the centre, not sure where to turn.

I spoke to my mentor about this and he simply asked me what I wanted to do. For me, the answer was clear. I wanted to do something I loved. I knew I could positively impact hundreds of lives and to do that I had to further develop the #GameChangers program. My mentor then asked me a question which will stick with me forever. All he asked was 'why aren't you doing that then?'

My answer was because I didn't want to upset anyone. He then highlighted to me that by being stuck in a state of limbo, I was actually upsetting both groups of people and further stalling the growth of the program. I was terrified of saying no to anyone for fear of upsetting them, and I was avoiding difficult conversations because they were awkward to have. By being constantly scared of criticism or judgement of my character, those very inhibitions were exactly what was holding me and the program back.

Steve Jobs once said "Your work is going to fill a large part of your life, and the only way to be truly satisfied is to do what you believe is great work. And the only way to do great work is to love what you do. If you haven't found it yet, keep looking. Don't settle." I had never resonated with this more. Therefore, I made the decision to prioritise the #GameChangers program over everything else and go all in.

Life tip: If you do anything in life, you are always going to be met with criticism. If you want to be ordinary, then you are going to be met with ordinary responses. When you step into the extraordinary and do something different, some people aren't going to be able to comprehend that, and you are going to experience extraordinary responses (both positive and negative). That's ok, because there will be a group of people who totally get what you do and why you do it, and they are the only people that matter.

And that brings me to today, where I have transformed the lives of hundreds of clients. I have found my true purpose and calling. It has been a journey filled with challenges, triumphs and unexpected twists. But through it all, one thing has remained constant – the unshakeable belief that with passion, determination and a willingness to adapt, anything is possible. Working out not only transformed my physique, but also my mental capabilities, which have profoundly changed my life and shaped this program. Without a doubt, I wouldn't be where I am today if I hadn't made the decision to pick up the weights. That's precisely why I'm committed to what I do now. I view it as a personal responsibility to unlock the potential of each member and empower them to assume complete control of their health and fitness indefinitely. For many of my clients, embarking on this journey is just the beginning, setting off a chain reaction. Once clients seize control of their health and fitness, newfound confidence radiates into every aspect of their lives, unlocking a side of life they never knew existed.

This is why I operate Future Bodies and the #GameChangers program in the way I do. I have designed this program to make a significant impact on my clients' lives, guiding them to their health and fitness goals once and for all, ensuring that they stay there and breaking the cycle of perpetual starting and stopping on their journey. Not only is this achieved by an incredibly supportive coaching team but also by surrounding clients with a phenomenally supportive community of like-minded individuals who share the same goals. This will be explored in greater detail later.

8. What Does Taking Control of Your Health and Fitness Mean?

Let's dive into what it truly means to be in the best shape of your life. But before we get stuck in, let me be upfront about something – if you're here solely for the promise of chiselled six-pack abs and bulging biceps, I kindly suggest you put this book down.

We're conditioned to believe that it means looking like a magazine cover model to be healthy, fit and strong. Having been in that world, I can promise you that that is not the best shape of your life. Let me share a little secret: many of those cover models you see are following incredibly strict, unsustainable diets for months just to get 'camera-ready'. And to top it off, their photos often undergo so much retouching that the end results are beyond reach for most of us. Moreover, the vast majority are on performance-enhancing drugs, which sets completely unrealistic and unattainable aspirations for the mainstream population.

My definition of being in the best shape of your life is being healthy, fit and strong, and having the confidence to tackle any of life's challenges head-on and with conviction. This isn't about walking around the beach with the posturing of a peacock. Being in the best shape of your life is completely unique and different for every client that I work with. It may be that you want to feel a certain way, perhaps you want to look a certain way, perhaps you want to move in a certain way. It's my job to get you to your definition of the best shape of your life.

Understanding your goals, however, is just one part of the puzzle. So, let's start with the fundamentals and take a closer look at a "typical" client I work with.

Imagine someone who has battled with their weight, health, fitness and mindset for a minimum of 5 years, and often much longer. They want to shed at least 10 kilograms and, despite their best efforts, they've repeatedly tried and failed to conquer their health and fitness challenges alone and are in the worst place they have ever been with their health and fitness.

Before joining my program, these clients find themselves trapped in an exhausting stop/start cycle that they just can't seem to break. They're fed up with the frustration of never gaining real momentum when it comes to their health and fitness.

The biggest hurdle that my potential clients face is that they've never found a sustainable solution that aligns with their lifestyle. They struggle to juggle the demands of social gatherings, a bustling career and/or a busy family life while trying to prioritise their well-being.

During my time as a coach, I have had the honour of working with people in all areas of life: directors of hugely successful businesses like Fortnum & Mason, winners of Crufts, self-employed tradespeople, busy mums, paraplegics, amputees, students, makeup artists, business owners... the list goes on. Every single one of those clients has achieved peak physical and mental health through my coaching philosophy.

Here's where our '21-Day Kickstart Program' steps in – a tailor-made program which breaks the stop/start cycle once and for all. So, when clients are ready to discover a sustainable path to health and fitness, they're in the right place with us and our program.

9. An Introduction to Coaching

All clients are guaranteed three key outcomes:

- You will be empowered to take total control of your health and fitness for good.
- You will feel able to stick to this program sustainably forever and even enjoy it!
- We will ensure that you get into the top 5% of the population in terms of health, fitness and strength.

Typically, the prospective clients we work with struggle with at least one of these issues:

- You feel stuck in a rut, caught in a cycle of starting and stopping your fitness journey, often ending up back where you started or sometimes in a worse off position.
- You are struggling to stay motivated to maintain exercise as a consistent part of your life, with it often slipping by the wayside.
- You are failing to find a long-term, enjoyable fitness solution that aligns with your lifestyle.

If you can resonate with any of these issues, then this book is for you!

The Discovery Call

Think back to chapter 1, when you stumble across a gym that offers coaching. You have booked your discovery call, and that is where your journey starts!

During the call, you discuss your objectives, past obstacles and why now is the right time to prioritise your health and fitness. You articulate your short-term goals and envision what success looks like for you.

Using a decision framework, the coach determines if they can genuinely help you. It is a common misconception that by booking a call and discussing your goals, you will automatically be offered a place on the '21-day kickstart program'. If we took on every prospective new client that we spoke to on the phone, then that would water down our offering and devalue our ability to change lives. The discovery call screens out any unsuitable candidates.

We have all been into gyms where there are ego lifters, or those who act as if they own it. They are intimidating and could quite possibly have put you off from ever wanting to step foot in a gym again. If I ever find myself on the call with somebody like that, then I politely disclose that we aren't the right gym for them and recommend them a few other options where they may be better suited.

If it is decided that you can be helped and that you are a good fit for the program, we really drill down into the nitty-gritty, and determine your motives and what you would need to achieve over the next 3 weeks to consider this kickstart program a huge success.

You are then prescribed a tailored solution to achieve your goals, consisting of a clear plan which is your roadmap to follow. The coach stresses to you that if you stick to that plan, you will achieve your goals without a doubt. Then, you discuss training frequencies, typically we recommend 2-3 sessions per week. Each session is personalised, with a coach ready to guide you through your workout. Unlimited support is emphasised, ensuring that you have all the help you need to succeed.

Non-negotiables are also outlined to you, because this coached approach is not about taking client's money and leaving them to do their own thing or not follow the layout of the program. To proceed with the discovery call, then there are certain rules that need to be addressed and agreed to. Those are:

1. You need to be happy to be held accountable to your goals on a weekly basis, and if you are not on track, to agree to be pulled up on this.

2. Most clients on the '21-day kickstart program' start with a fat loss phase to their approach. For this to be done successfully, you would need to be happy to follow your specific nutritional plan that fits perfectly around your existing lifestyle and family arrangements.

This includes going out for dinner and having a drink too! Additionally, you need to agree to track on an app whatever you eat and drink, to give full visibility on your calorie and macros intake.

3. You will also be expected to confirm that you will definitely be able to make the time to work out around 2-3 times per week.

Provided you are happy with these three non-negotiable stipulations, and after confirming your understanding and agreement, the conversation moves on to discussing the community aspect.

You are informed that you will be surrounded by an incredible community of like-minded individuals, who have all been in your shoes once. Some will have only been on the program for a matter of weeks, opposed to others who have been on the program for 4+ years. Wherever they are on their own journeys, you will always be welcomed with open arms.

Once everything is agreed upon, understood and any questions you may have are answered, you are offered a place on the '21-day kickstart program'. Excited, you confirm your decision, and your start date is scheduled, which is often immediately if that fits with your plans.

There's still some administrative work to be done, such as sort payment for the initial kickstart program and sending over a legally binding document which needs to be signed that day. This clearly outlines the roles and responsibilities of the coaching team, but also the roles and responsibility that is expected of you as a fully-fledged client. The document also protects us both from any legal matters that may arise, but its main purpose is to explain in black and white how you can get the very best out of working with the coaching team.

Additionally, 4+ hours of pre-learning material is provided to you. This is for you to watch before you even step foot in the gym and is designed to familiarise yourself with the program before your first session, and answer specifically any and every question you may have. In the pre-learning we cover how best to manage your nutrition, how to eat when out and about, how to book your sessions with us, how to contact us; basically this is the one stop shop for everything that you need to know to achieve the very best results with us. You are then booked in for your first 'onboarding session'.

Onboarding Session

You arrive at the gym on the designated day, and you are going to meet one of the team who is going to take you through a full health assessment. There is a special set of scales at the gym, which analyses your body in detail. It looks at many variables, including but not limited to levels of body fat and visceral fat, your metabolic age and your hydration levels. This gives an initial health start point, and so there is absolutely zero ambiguity on where you are starting. This process needs to be repeated weekly to accurately track your progress on a biometric level.

Following on from the biometric assessment, you receive a comprehensive gym tour. You are introduced to a private studio where your workouts will take place, away from the main gym floor, with no big windows or viewing platforms for other people to watch, just cool equipment and funky lighting. It is a private space for coaching clients, and coaching clients only.

It is in that studio that the coach then takes you through your initial movement screening, which enables friendly analysis of your key movement patterns. This allows the coach to discover if you have any issues with mobility or flexibility that may impede your training. This is then followed by a short strength and fitness test, establishing your fitness baseline. This is not as scary as it sounds though, I promise! By the end of this onboarding session, your coach is now fully aware of your capabilities, your start point from a health perspective and exactly how fit and strong you already are.

Heading back to the consultation room, you have a chat with your coach who answers any questions that you may have. They go through your results with you and ensure that you have full understanding of everything so far. The session will not be finished until you are totally happy. Your first proper #GameChangers session is scheduled and you bid farewell.

Following the onboarding session, you receive a message from your success coach, checking in with you to make sure you are okay, aren't feeling too overwhelmed, and to answer any questions which you may have. These questions get answered within 24 hours.

Your '21-Day Kickstart Program'

You then attend your first proper session a few days later, commonly on a Monday, and it goes seamlessly. You are met by a coach that you haven't met yet, and you panic slightly because you don't know their name. Your fears are put to bed quickly as the coach walks over, introduces themselves and greets you by your first name and welcomes you to your first session. They explain that they have seen the training notes that were made during your onboarding session and they know exactly at what point you are.

You go into the studio and are introduced to a group of like-minded people, and the session layout is explained. You notice that everyone does a slightly different workout, depending on how long they have been on the program, in line with their fitness levels.

The warm up commences, targeting specific muscle groups which you are about to work. The main workout then begins, and you are coached every step of the way over the next 60 minutes. There is great motivational music throughout, and you feel constantly checked in on, making sure you are happy and comfortable. In between rest stations, you notice that everyone is laughing and bantering with each other, with nobody taking any notice of how sweaty or red someone may have gone! In fact, you don't feel any judgement and dare you say it, you may have actually enjoyed yourself. At the end of the session, the coach writes down everybody's scores on the whiteboard so when you revisit that session later on in the week, you know what you need to beat! The session proceeds into a cool down, with specific stretches to loosen any tired muscles. You go home feeling fulfilled, excited and probably a bit achy! You are then contacted again after the session, to make sure you are happy, know what you are doing and that any concerns you may have are addressed. This personalised experience sets you up for success, with ongoing support and guidance tailored to your needs and goals.

Fast forward 21 days and you have been continually checked in with, you have been taken through your workouts step by step, and we have constantly updated you on your progress so you know that exactly what you are doing is working. Alongside this, you will have experienced unwavering and unlimited professional support. Once you have finished your 'kickstart program', you are ready to book in a 'further goal planning' session with a member of the coaching team. This session plans your future health and fitness goals, using a crystal clear roadmap to ensure that these happen, and enables you to obtain an understanding of our tiered pricing structure, based on the most suitable option for you.

Can you see the stark contrast between a typical gym membership which sets you up for failure from the offset and this coached approach?

10. The Coaching Journey

A typical client journey unfolds in three dynamic phases, each designed to ignite your transformation:

Foundation Stage – Kickstart

As discussed in the previous chapter, this is where all clients start on their 21-day transformative journey following your discovery call.

Acceleration Phase – Fat Loss and Getting Healthy

This stage is where we have really nailed down the fundamentals of what needs to be in place to drive long-term sustainable change. At the end of the kickstart program, we conduct a 'further goal planning' session where we can really dial in on what worked well on the program for you, and what didn't work quite so well. This allows us to fine tune our approach and accelerate the client's results.

We start to open up the client's mind on why they are here and what they want to achieve. Every client must get healthy first. Fundamentally, we want to ensure that our clients are no longer at an elevated risk of cancer, diabetes, strokes and heart attacks – basically, all the nasty things that keep us awake at night. We want to ensure that our clients are at the lowest risk possible. Typically, this means that for gents the target is to drop below the 20% body fat mark, while the ladies aim for a minimum of 30% body fat. The sole objective here is to get my clients healthy before they start to elevate their lifestyle to new heights of achievement. This phase lays the groundwork for their health and vitality journey, paving the way for what's to come.

Elevation Phase

This phase is where we supersede all expectations of what was thought possible. Once our clients have become healthy, fit and strong, I see it as our responsibility to continue to elevate their journey. It's our job as coaches to show our clients how far they can go. The journey doesn't end – it evolves. Enter the Elevation Phase.

For the record, I don't mean bulging biceps and washboard abs. I mean getting dads to a place where they feel confident to take their top off at the beach and play with their kids wholeheartedly, without worrying what people are thinking about them, or for mums to walk back into the workplace with the confidence they deserve, allowing them to be an incredible role model to their kids.

Here, it's all about fine-tuning and making incremental improvements while keeping our clients' health and fitness at peak levels, unlocking their true potential. Clients can say goodbye to frustrating stop/start cycles, as this phase is about maintaining their newfound vitality for the long haul.

I have developed a system, aiming to get all of our clients into the top 5% of their population for being healthy, fit and strong. We can take you all the way to an athletic level of performance when it comes to your health and fitness. A specific set of criteria has been developed, particular to each client and their goals, age and gender, which assesses your levels of fitness and strength, and grades you on a scale. This is across a broad spectrum of exercises, with targets being set for your cardiovascular fitness, bench press, squat, deadlifts, pull ups (or variations of) and other various tests. As you get stronger/fitter, the targets get more and more challenging, and you can see your progress with every test that we run. We refer to this test as the 'Strength and Fitness Test' which occurs biannually. This will be expanded upon in Chapter 18.

A large proportion of our clients are successful for grading in the top 5% as a minimum. You wouldn't believe how fit, strong and capable some of our clients are. Even now, 16 years in, it never ceases to amaze me just how strong and fit people can get. In fact, we now have many clients who are in the top 2% of their populations for being healthy, fit and strong, all whilst holding down demanding jobs, being parents and having social lives!

So, whether you're at the beginning of your journey or looking to sustain your peak condition, my three-phase approach will guide you every step of the way.

Now that you understand what it means to be in the best shape of your life and how that definition varies for every client, we need to delve into how to achieve the very best results.

11. Start With Your Deep Meaningful Why?

To drive lasting change, you must start with your true why. This is your calling. It could be related to health, feeling tired of your clothes feeling tight, or perhaps feeling unfit and lacking confidence. Maybe you're feeling unmotivated, just coasting through life without a real sense of purpose. You need to dig deeper than these surface reasons. Your deep and meaningful why is where you want to be and why it is so important to you.

My 'why' is that I want to be an incredible role model to my children, partner and clients. I strive to be fit, strong and healthy, performing at my best in all areas of my life. For you, your reasons may be entirely different, and that's perfectly okay!

You need to understand your why. Perhaps, you want to have the confidence to speak up in your workplace, or even just to tighten up and be at the top of your game – your why is personal to you and you alone. Everyone has a trigger point. For example, this could be that you can't or don't participate in the sports day parents' race because you are simply not fit enough. This moment stops you in your tracks. You vow from that moment, something needs to change, so you take a breath and think that now is the right time to take control of your health and fitness.

I would like you to take a moment and imagine yourself 2-3 years from now. What does that look like? Have the scales decreased by 10kg? Are you waking up each day feeling energised with a spring in your step? Have you finally gained the confidence to deal with the issue that you have been putting off? What do you need to achieve in 2-3 years from now to chalk this program up as a massive success?

Exercise:

I'd like you to grab a pen and a piece of paper or open up the notes section on your phone. Write down your top three biggest health and fitness goals you would like to achieve within the next 2-3 years. These goals should be ones that currently, you can't pursue because your health and fitness isn't where you would like it to be.

Once you have clearly identified what you truly want to achieve, you're stepping into the world of making lasting, positive change! Once we have clarity on your *why*, we then dive into *how*...

12. The 5 Key Pillars of Success

We focus on **five** KEY areas to drive lasting change.

1. The Plan

Based upon your long-term future goals, we devise a plan that then becomes your crystal-clear road map to follow. This roadmap ensures you WILL achieve your goals. *Guaranteed.*

- This plan involves the minimum exercise commitment per week and what type of exercises you should be doing
- What you need to do nutritionally to achieve your goals
- What you need to drink each day to be sufficiently hydrated
- What your non-negotiables each day are, which all must happen to move the needle in the right direction

2. The Training

We then design the right training solution that fits perfectly around your lifestyle, but you have to enjoy it! If you don't enjoy it, then guess what? You won't stick to it.

We focus on three key areas of session design with clients.

Firstly, strength is prioritised, followed by accessory and finally conditioning, which is cardiovascular fitness and health. Our training sessions are designed to be progressive, fun, slightly competitive and with a community where you can have a laugh with the coaches and fellow clients. We also ensure that we can be completely flexible around you and your lifestyle.

3. The Support

There is never a cap on the level of support we offer clients. All prospective clients need to know that we are here to provide you with all the support you could ever need to take total control of your health and fitness. This can vary from weekly one-on-one check-ins, Zoom calls, additional gym time, or working with additional professionals. Many of our clients suffer with a condition or ailment that we need to be aware of. For example, let's say we are working with a client who has compressed vertebrae. It's imperative that a) we know about it in the first place, and b) what other health professionals are doing to help, so that we know how we can complement their treatment plan. It is our responsibility to support you on an individualised basis, and this comes as standard.

4. The Accountability

As coaches, it is our job to hold you accountable. We hold you accountable in the three main areas:

- Your goals – We need to review your progress regularly to ensure that you are on track to achieving your goals with us.

- Your nutrition – We check in and review your nutrition which has been specifically structured to you, your lifestyle and your dietary requirements, to ensure you are eating the right things to achieve your goals with us. We make tweaks and changes as and when required, such as increase protein intake or decrease fats.

- Your exercise – We hold you accountable to your exercise commitments by tracking how many sessions you book in each week, the intensity of your workouts, and alter if necessary. Additionally, if you have booked in a session but do not arrive, you receive a friendly check in from a member of the team to, most importantly, make sure you are okay, but to also remind you to book your next sessions in so you do not lose momentum or progress. Furthermore, if you haven't booked your sessions in for the week, and you haven't given a reason, such as you are away on holiday, then you can expect a friendly reminder to get them booked in promptly.

The role of a coach is to hold you accountable. A good coach isn't afraid to call out a poor excuse and it is our job to help. We do that by trying to deal with any issues that are holding you back head on.

Critical, objective feedback is the single most important factor when it comes to accountability. We often shy away from exposure, from criticism, because it can hurt our feelings. In the coaching contract signed by any client who joins the program, it states that you must be happy to accept critical feedback. It is easy to let life get in the way, but ultimately your results are all that matters. We hold you accountable to your goals, and it's our job to make sure that they happen by ensuring that you stick to the program long enough for it to have a massive positive impact on your life, enabling you to change deep-rooted habits and implement new healthier ones.

5. The Community

Environment dictates performance, and your tribe is one of the most important and often overlooked factors in your health and fitness journey. Motivational speaker Jim Rohn famously stated that "we are the average of the five people we spend the most time with." If you are overweight, the chances are your friends are too. If you live an unhealthy lifestyle by drinking excessively or taking drugs, the same. Surround yourself with people who are motivating, encouraging and your role models! Our community is discussed at length in Chapter 15.

13. Your Back Pocket

When working with us, it is absolutely vital that you feel informed and that you are on track towards your goals at all times. If you lack direction or certainty, it's essential that we provide you with the feedback and adaptations to your plan so you know you are progressing towards your goals.

We are available to assist you 365 days a year, and you have us in your back pocket. With the use of our specialised app, you can message us, ask us questions, book in calls or ask for more specific help. We also have several processes in place to help you, because sometimes you may be veering off track without even noticing.

Ultimately, you are paying us for results and our expertise, so it's crucial that you understand the outcomes you are focused on and how we plan to help you achieve them. We employ various feedback methods to ensure clear communication and tracking of your progress.

The Weekly Checklist

Every Sunday and Monday, you receive a message from the coaching team to ensure that you know exactly what you need to do for the upcoming week. You will also be advised on whether you are due for a one-on-one check-in with a coach, where we can assess your progress.

You are also reminded to:

- Book and attend 2-3 gym sessions per week (ideally)
- Track everything you eat and drink
- Drink approximately 1 litre of water per 25 kilograms of body weight
- Weigh in on the scales and track your progress weekly
- Meet your exercise requirements outside of your gym sessions and ensure you are working hard enough in those sessions

Additionally, we enquire about how you're doing overall and if you have any questions or if there is anything else that we can assist with.

The Traffic Light System

We also operate what's called a traffic light system. This system follows three very specific criteria. In any interaction we have with you, you should always feel like you know exactly what you should be focusing on, what your goals are and how you are going to achieve them. However, as days turn into weeks and weeks into months, it's easy for you to start losing focus or feeling slightly lost as you progress towards your goals and lose visibility on how far you have come.

We call it the #GameChangers phenomenon, where clients

don't feel like they are doing very well or progressing in the right direction, however, in reality they are crushing their health and fitness goals. One of the drawbacks of being in an incredibly successful coaching program is that when everyone around you is equally progressing, it's hard not to compare against fellow #GameChangers who have been doing it a lot longer than you. It is actually quite common for clients to feel like they are treading water or regressing on their goals when, in fact, they're making progress and just need to continue as they are.

It's our job as coaches to ascertain exactly where you are at and give guidance accordingly, and so we have the traffic light system. This is a simple yet highly effective tool, as by being proactive any potential issues can be addressed before they become active problems.

We ask every client to review their own progress on a weekly basis via the app. It takes 30 seconds, and they literally select green, amber or red depending on how they feel.

Clients select green if:

- They are happy with where they are
- They are making good progress
- They are focused on their goals and are on track to achieve them

- They have no concerns currently

Clients select amber if:

- They feel that everything is going ok, but feel like things could be better
- They feel that perhaps their progress is stalling

Amber clients are advised to message the coaching team via the app explaining their concerns, and a member of the team will get back to them within 24 hours.

Clients select red if:

- They feel completely lost and confused about their goals or progress
- They feel like giving up

A red client could occur because they may have ignored the amber phase and buried their head in the sand before realising that they are totally lost. It could also be due to a significant life event which has totally thrown them. Every client could find themselves in the red zone, so this traffic light system is crucial for maintaining positive momentum. Red clients book in a check in call and discuss their problems or concerns with a coach, and a solution is found together.

The Quarterly Review

Every 90 days, we conduct one-on-one quarterly reviews

where we turbocharge your progress and propel you toward your goals with precision. During these sessions, we dive deep to uncover what's working for you, what needs a tweak, and together we craft a bulletproof strategy to smash through every single one of your health and fitness milestones. We delve into the key areas that we know you need to focus on to make your goals happen.

We review your average weekly session attendance, examine your time management, assess how hard you work in sessions, evaluate how well you track and manage your nutrition, scrutinise your hydration levels, gauge how on track you feel toward your goals and assess various physical metrics, including body fat levels, muscle mass, hydration percentage, metabolic age and bodyweight on the scales. We also review your strength and fitness progress to ensure it aligns with your objectives. Based on these metrics, we pinpoint specific areas to tweak your weekly and daily approach to accelerate your progress.

We discuss topics such as improving session frequency (if needed), evaluating the effectiveness of your workout approach, optimising time management, suggesting nutritional tweaks and assessing your progress toward your long-term health and fitness goals.

These sessions ensure that you are clear on what you need to do and how you can enhance your approach to accelerate your progress toward your goals. At the end of each appointment, every client leaves with a custom battle plan tailored to their life and goals to be a little bit better than they were 90 days previously.

It takes time to deliver life-changing results, and small lifestyle changes are key. If we were to completely overhaul your lifestyle from the outset, it would be overwhelming and likely lead to resistance from partners, family members, work and social circles. Instead, when we first start with a client, we make minor tweaks to their lifestyle to begin moving the needle with minimal impact. Then, every 90 days, we make small, often imperceptible, adjustments following the 1% rule. Continuously aiming to be 1% better each week has a massive impact on health, strength and fitness over the course of 12 months and further years. These changes, implemented gradually, eventually propel you toward your goals at a pace you never thought possible. At the end of these quarterly reviews, we ensure that you are absolutely zeroed in and focused on your goals, and leave you with a custom plan in place to ensure you're on the right path to success.

The Ad Hoc Check In

We also reach out to clients that we haven't heard from or seen in a while. During each team meeting, we sit down to review our clients' progress and if somebody's name comes up due to an injury, or perhaps they seemed down in a session, we reach out to them as soon as possible to check in and make sure they are okay. We prioritise support for our clients, and there's no limit to the amount of support they get. We're always in your corner, every step of the way, and sometimes all it takes is a little nudge from a coach to open up so we can get you back on the right track.

14. The Stages of Maslow's Hierarchy of Needs

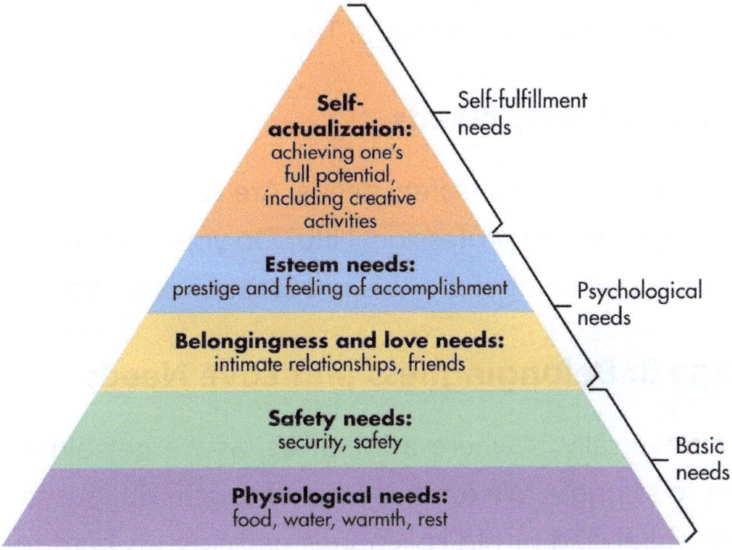

McLeod, S. (2018).
Maslow's Hierarchy of Needs. Simply Psychology.

Now, I don't want to get too heavy on the psychology here, however, let's look at Maslow's Hierarchy of Needs to give us a broad overview of what we need to fulfil your physiological and psychological drives to ensure that you stick to the program. While this theory has its limitations, I believe it serves as a great benchmark for understanding basic human psychology and gives us a platform to understand our psychological and physiological needs on a primal level.

Stage 1: Physiological Needs

You need food, water, warmth and rest to sustain basic life functions. For a typical client, you have enough food – often in surplus. There is unlimited water and you have a warm bed to sleep in at night. Tick!

Stage 2: Safety Needs

You then have your safety needs. Are you safe and secure in your home and professional life? Do you feel safe in your surroundings? Hopefully, this is another tick for you.

Stage 3: Belongingness and Love Needs

This typically is where a lot of us, as we get older, can start to struggle. We often fall out of touch with our friends from childhood or old colleagues perhaps. It's hard to feel part of a community when you have such little time, and everyone has so many different needs and wants. Trying to form a common goal can be tough. Therefore, we can find ourselves seeking new friendships, approval, or recognition from others. I absolutely hold my hands up here and say that I have experienced this firsthand and it is hard to have a sense of belonging. However, what is important to note is that this is normal, it's okay, and it will happen repeatedly throughout your life.

If you are lucky, typically your love needs are met from your partner, your family, close friends and even pets!

Stage 4: Esteem Needs

Often, we work with clients who have achieved a lot in their lives, either professionally or personally, and thus feel a sense of achievement. Nevertheless, many clients often feel like they could achieve so much more with their health and fitness, and don't feel any positive sense of achievement within their own bodies. If this sounds like you, do not worry, as this is often the case with new starters. We can step in and give you the tools and performance metrics to ensure that you know that what you are doing is going to get you to your goals.

Each and every week, we monitor your progress and continue to elevate to improve your health and fitness. At this point, you are also going to really start to see the benefits of exercise and get that spring back in your step.

Stage 5: Self-Actualisation Needs

Achieving your known or unknown potential, including creative activities, is exactly what our coaching program is about. It's about enabling you to take total control of your health and fitness, achieve your initial goals and then embark on a journey to explore what you can achieve with your health and fitness. By having the top 5% and above of the population as a target, this feeds into your self-actualisation needs that perhaps you never knew you had before. These goals push you to explore your fitness journey, striving to be better than the previous day, continuously.

15. The Power of Community

The power of community when it comes to taking control of your health and fitness cannot be overstated. The strength of a gym community will single-handedly dictate whether you will go on to achieve your health and fitness goals or not.

Before we delve into the importance of a gym community, I want to explore how we typically form friendships and communities from early childhood and work our way up to the present day. Bear with me here – there is a method to my madness.

Childhood Friendships & Community

I'd like you to take a moment to think back to your childhood. How did we make friends at school? We often shared similar values or interests, whether it was sports, fashion or toys. We then talked about those shared interests because we were genuinely interested in them. Over time, we spent more time together, sharing experiences like lessons, lunch breaks and after-school clubs.

As time went on, we developed a mutual understanding, and typically, friendships formed in small group settings. Many of these friendships last years. Earlier in this book I mentioned my mate Chris, a perfect example of just this!

Workplace Friendships & Community

Now let's apply this to the workplace. I bet that some of your closest relationships are with your colleagues, right? You spend a significant amount of time with them, typically around 8 hours a day. You share common practices and interests related to your workplace, and you go through work-related trials and tribulations together, alongside an element of teamwork and camaraderie that you experience daily.

As you interact with various people, you'll eventually find someone or a group of people at work with whom you just 'click' with. It is likely there are also social occasions that you get invited to through work connections. Before you know it, you've found someone you can really relate to, someone you can talk to about common interests and shared experiences. Et voilà! You've extended your social circle and made new friends.

Sport Friendships & Community

Joining a local sports team when moving to a new area is a great example. You're likely to find shared common interests and values among your teammates. As you go through the experiences of training and playing matches together, facing challenges and victories as a team, you'll naturally form connections. With exposure to multiple people in the team, you're bound to connect with some of them and develop friendships along the way. It's all about shared experiences and the bonds that form through them.

#GameChangers Friendships & Community

I have developed the #GameChangers program based on what I have perceived to be lacking in society, and what I believe should be more prevalent across various aspects of life.

Whilst we're constantly connected through the internet, we've seemingly lost the ability to forge new friendships. Paradoxically, despite this heightened connectivity, many of us feel more isolated than ever before.

I have naturally outgrown numerous friendship circles, and I don't regret any of it. Those peer groups would have ultimately hindered my progress in both personal and professional life. However, that doesn't mean it hasn't been a profoundly lonely journey at times. I have also been part of many groups with business owners in similar positions. In these supportive environments, surrounded by like-minded individuals with similar goals, something amazing happens. You feel connected, and your ideas flow, rather than being met with incomprehension from peers who have no idea of the challenges you face. When you walk the well-trodden path of other trail blazers and see success all around you, you can't help but feel motivated and uplifted.

And so, when looking to start something new or achieve

something that you haven't done before, it is absolutely vital that you spend time with the right people who are there to uplift and propel you towards those goals.

Communities are vital, and our coaching program provides both a physical and online community for all of our clients. As much as we like to think we aren't social beings and that we are independent – with many often wearing this as a badge of honour – we are social creatures by nature and thrive off social interactions and acceptance within a community. If we tie that in with a common goal, we are creating an incredible program that will elevate your results more than you could ever have imagined. Our community is unrivalled in what we do. Surrounding yourself with winners is a must when starting out on your health and fitness journey, and consequently also enhances your own sense of belonging in Maslow's Hierarchy of Needs.

Whilst you are focusing on your individual goals, there is still a significant element of teamwork as you are in the same coaching room, doing very similar workouts tailored to your ability. You also face the same barriers to progress as everyone else in the room: time constraints, childcare issues, work commitments, stress, to name but a few. You share commonalities and camaraderie across many key areas.

Combine this with being in an incredibly supportive environment, and you can't help but form friendships while you are on our program. We have clients who have quite literally formed friendships for life by joining this program, and it's one of the many things that make me incredibly proud to do what I do. Sure, we need to be bloody good coaches and know how to bring out your best, but by weaving in an unstoppable community of like-minded individuals, you will be able to take your health and fitness to heights you could never have imagined.

16. Choose Your Community Wisely

Being surrounded by the right community is absolutely vital to your success. Below I am going to outline some true interactions I have had with previous peer groups. Scenarios A & B are conversations I have had with people who want to know about my business and future aspirations.

Scenario A:

"Be careful you don't get too big. Running a business is really hard, why do you bother doing it? Surely it's not worth it? You must be careful that you don't become too commercial."

Opposed to...

Scenario B:

"Josh, that sounds great! How are you planning on getting there? How are you going to make it happen? How are you going to find balance with your family life whilst pursuing your goals?"

Or let's look at Scenarios C & D, which are from conversations about my focus on my health and fitness. Bear in mind I was 19% body fat at the time, a healthy percentage.

Scenario C:

"Be careful, Josh, you are looking skinny. Why do you track everything, isn't it a little obsessive? You're in decent shape as it is, why do you still put so much focus into it?"

Opposed to...

Scenario D:

"Josh, you are looking good! What are your goals with your health and fitness? I struggle to track my foods, how do you maintain discipline?"

Can you see how Scenarios A & C above were simply meant to hold me back? They were coming from someone who was uneducated in those areas, and their questioning could purely be based upon their own insecurities. The questioning wasn't about me or why I was doing those things, it was merely about protecting their ego.

These types of comments say everything about the mindset of the individual asking the questions. These types of people are not conducive to your progress, and you need to avoid them as best as you can.

Surrounding yourself with the right peer group is absolutely essential when it comes to changing your life and taking control of your health and fitness. You need to be surrounded by those who have done or are doing exactly what you're thinking of doing. You need to be surrounded by their success, which you can use as motivation to level up your own game.

In each coaching session, there is a coach leading the session who has quite literally been there and done it with their health and fitness (all of our coaches go through the same training and accreditation as our clients). They also know everyone's capability and ensure that everyone in the room knows exactly what they are doing and what they are striving to achieve. Every session, our coaches make sure you are on target to make that goal happen.

We have clients regularly hitting their personal bests in sessions with us. That only happens, however, by having a crystal-clear plan of where they want to be, being held accountable by coaches and having performance metrics in place, whilst being alongside an incredible community who encourage and motivate each other to achieve their potential.

17. Community Events = Friendships for Life

Alongside group coaching sessions to build a strong community of like-minded individuals, we also provide and integrate a jam-packed social calendar which helps to nurture bonds outside of the gym space and further bring out your best. This actively opens up conversations with fellow clients, all of whom now have a common ground. In these social settings, friendships are made. We have clients that go away on holiday together and regularly meet for coffee after their workouts.

Let's look at a couple of case studies on how we build these lifelong friendships:

Case Study 1: Scafell Pike & Honister Bridge

We took our clients to conquer Scafell Pike, England's highest peak, in April 2024. The group of clients was varied, ranging from stay-at-home parents to business owners, all ageing between 21 and 64. We were away from Friday to Sunday, and we organised car sharing to foster friendships among clients with similar personalities and interests. On the way up, we initiated a series of team-building games to enhance camaraderie.

This started with a WhatsApp group, and each vehicle had a nominated chief note-taker and answerer. We then posed questions and tasks to make the 8-hour journey from Devon to the Lake District more enjoyable, encouraging conversations and team bonding. Setting the tone for teamwork from the outset was essential. As cliché as it sounds, we believe in the strength of unity, and fostering a sense of community was our goal for the weekend.

Unfortunately, the weather was dreadful, with Storm Katherine raging at full force, bringing anticipated wind speeds of over 80mph and endless rain. Such conditions would have made hiking unsafe, necessitating a switch to plan B if they persisted. Luckily, the weather played ball and by 8am on the Saturday, we were out the door, en route to meet our mountain leaders.

Accompanied by four mountain leaders, we tackled different routes up to Scafell Pike, ranging from slightly easier and shorter to longer more exposed paths involving scrambling up the rock face, but planned to meet near the top in order to summit and descend as a group.

With no phone signal and only the people you're with, you're momentarily detached from life's day-to-day distractions. As time went on, clients naturally opened up, sharing about their past, present and future aspirations. Over the 7-hour walk, clients revealed personal stories they hadn't shared before, creating a profound bond among the group.

The view from the top was absolutely incredible. We

didn't linger long due to strong winds, but we managed to snap a team photo with the banner before heading down to find a sheltered spot for lunch. Once we made it down, we stopped at a nearby pub for a celebratory drink. Clients split into groups, discussing the hike and various life experiences. Upon arrival back at the hotel, conversations continued to flow into the evening. After dinner, clients dispersed into different rooms and groups, with some playing beer pong while others relaxed in the lounge with newfound friends.

For all of our weekend getaways, we aim to combine physical challenges with tests of mindset and psychological resilience. The latter occurred on the Sunday. Honister Bridge, a narrow wire bridge suspended 1,000 feet between rock faces, seemed perfect. Participants are securely strapped to a safety line and must inch their way across the flimsy, unstable bridge below.

Unfortunately, we couldn't evade the weather any longer, and we had to cancel the Honister Bridge activity. However, the venue was fantastic and offered us an indoor caving experience instead, which turned out to be perfect for our group.

We suited up in harnesses and ventured 100 metres inside the cave, navigating through climbing, ladder climbing and zip-lining through the mine shaft. It was an exhilarating morning that further fostered teamwork and camaraderie among the group. Afterwards, we all had a coffee and a cake, whilst talking about our experience before preparing to head back home.

Can you see the power of community and how friendships for life can be forged during weekends like this?

Case Study 2: Summer Social

Another example of a community event is our summer social. I may be biased, but the summer socials are just fantastic! It's held in a field or a barn, and we put on activities for the whole family. On offer is a variety of activities such as table tennis, swing ball, archery, kids activities, air rifle and air pistol competitions. We provide a barbeque for everyone, and there's also a bar where parents can relax whilst their children play, creating a day designed for the whole family to unwind and relax outside of a gym environment. We often find that many of our clients have similar lifestyles and commonalities, and events like this are a great way to help them form stronger bonds, social connections and friendships.

Of course, it wouldn't be a #GameChangers event without a little rivalry, so we hold a few competitions throughout the day, like the best archer and the best air rifle score, and a giant game of rounders! This of course gets rather competitive!

Case Study 3: Black Tie Awards Ceremony

Each year, we host a Black Tie Awards Ceremony for our clients. It's the biggest event of the year, and it's an absolute blast. We also have photographers and videographers there capturing the essence of the night, giving us lasting memories.

The ceremony is about celebrating clients' successes on the program. For some, this means losing their target weight. For others, it's qualifying for the top 2% of their populations in terms of their health, fitness and strength, a goal in which they've worked towards for numerous years.

There's a black tie dress code, food and drink is provided and there is an arranged seating plan. There are games, speeches and awards. It's an incredible evening designed to highlight every single client's success, no matter how big or small. We want every client to feel like the rockstar they are.

The night is engineered to showcase everyone's true potential and demonstrate to our community what is possible on this program. Some clients have only been with us a couple of months and just getting started on their journey, whilst others have achieved more than they ever thought possible. For those new clients, it's an amazing opportunity to see how far they can take their health and fitness. Conversely, it's also a chance for our long-standing clients to reflect on their journey and appreciate how far they've come.

Throughout the night, we hand out awards for clients who have qualified for the top 5%, top 4%, top 3%, top 2% and top 1% of their populations. We call them up on stage, celebrate with speeches and blow the roof off the event. Additionally, we also present especially significant 'Coaches' Choice Awards' to members who have really stood out, such as:

- The Biggest Team Player
- Most Outstanding Progress
- Most Competitive Couple
- Biggest Transformation
- Biggest Inspiration
- Hall of Fame

Once dinner is finished and the awards are handed out, speeches conclude the formalities before the music kicks in. One year, however, members hijacked the stage and gave the coaches awards! It was truly amazing, and to this day, I feel incredibly privileged to have experienced that night with our coaching team. This event is some of the proudest memories I have as a coach. Seeing so many clients clapping, cheering and genuinely caring for each other is what motivates me every day to further develop and enhance the coaching experience for our clients.

The community aspect of this event is absolutely incredible. Lifelong friendships are made, tears are shed, laughter echoes through the venue and clients even ask for the date of next year's event so they can mark it in their diaries and plan whom they'd like to sit next to.

Can you now start to understand why it's so important to have a community that aligns with your goals to ensure your success?

To summarise, we've explored how friendships and communities are formed from early childhood up until now, and we've also looked at how we create those incredible friendships and communities on the program.

Creating an unstoppable community of like-minded individuals who are dedicated to becoming the best versions of themselves in a supportive environment, leads to remarkable outcomes. When everyone is focused on reaching their goals, supported by positive vibes and expert coaching, and when you genuinely enjoy spending your time with these individuals, something magical occurs. You not only witness weekly and monthly progress, but you also develop new friendships along the way. In this environment, you have absolute confidence that you're on the right path to achieving your goals.

You then become part of the minority of gym members

who successfully achieve their fitness objectives. There are no ifs, no buts and no maybes. We have had clients who struggled to walk now running half-marathons. We have ex-rugby players who were told they could never weight train again lifting two times their body weight safely. We have mums who thought they would never wear a bikini again in public booking holidays as a reward for achieving their goals. In this program, you will achieve your goals once and for all. This is why surrounding yourself with the right community is absolutely vital to your long-term success in achieving your health and fitness goals.

Can you see how these experiences create a sense of belonging, more than a generic gym does where you just pay for your membership and come and run on a treadmill?

18. Strength and Fitness Testing

As discussed earlier in the book, we have developed a grading system for clients to continually push themselves to become in the top 5% of their population for being healthy, fit and strong. This is tested biannually, allowing you to see firsthand where you are on your journey.

These testing weeks typically occur in June and November, and our regular coaching sessions are replaced with the strength and fitness tests. We aim to gather everyone together on a Saturday for group testing. The atmosphere is electric as everyone strives to beat their personal best from the last testing period. This friendly yet competitive environment brings out everyone's best, whether they've been on the program for a while or have just started. It's an amazing event that showcases how far you can take your health and fitness in a sustainable and healthy way.

As mentioned, we have developed a set of criteria, specific to each client and their specific goals, age and gender, which assesses your levels of fitness and strength and grades you on a scale. This is across a broad spectrum of exercises, with targets being set for your cardiovascular fitness, bench press, squat, deadlifts, pull ups (or variations of) and other various tests. As you get stronger/fitter, the targets get more and more challenging, and you can see your progress with every test that we run.

The power of the community cannot be underestimated. Trying to do the strength and fitness tests by yourself would never generate the improvements we see in our program, nor would it create the excitement and anticipation surrounding the tests. Everyone has their own goals based on age and gender, but they all support and motivate each other, standing shoulder to shoulder.

At the end of the strength and fitness testing weeks, we compile everyone's results. The June tests serve as pre-qualifiers for the November tests and allow you to know what you need to improve upon to score highly in November. November is where we evaluate your hard work, and the scores you achieve will determine if you qualify for the top 5% or above of the population or not. If you have, then you will be receiving an award at the Black Tie Awards Ceremony in December. If you don't qualify, then you will receive a full report on what needs to be improved upon to help you qualify next year.

19. Fixed Mindset Vs Growth Mindset

To achieve your potential and reach your goals, we need to fully understand two types of different mindsets:

Fixed mindset:

The belief that one's intelligence remains constant. Individuals with a fixed mindset might express sentiments such as:

- "I believe personal change is impossible."
- "I feel it's too late for most to learn and grow."
- "Constructive criticism feels like a personal attack to me."
- "I am unchangeable, there's no room for improvement."
- "I quit when faced with difficulty."

Growth mindset:

The belief that intelligence and abilities can be enhanced through dedication and education. Individuals with a growth mindset might express sentiments like:

- "I'm confident everyone can acquire new skills and excel with time."

- "Even if failure seems imminent, I persist because it's a chance to grow."
- "My improvement depends on the effort I invest, there's always room for growth."
- "Learning is perpetual, there's always something new to discover."

Can you see how these two approaches can determine your success? An individual who has a fixed mindset is content with their current situation, or doesn't believe that they can change. Therefore, they accept their circumstances without questioning, and don't consider bigger possibilities. Often, these individuals may not even realise their mindset. If you refer back to Scenarios A and C, on pages 88 and 89, these are examples of having a fixed mindset.

Compare this to a growth mindset, where individuals who have it believe that intelligence and talents can be improved through effort, learning and sheer determination (refer to Scenarios B and D). Could you imagine the possibilities if there were more people with a growth mindset in the world?

Often, when clients first reach out, they're stuck in the fixed mindset trap. They've tried and failed many times before, convincing themselves that they can't progress toward their health and fitness goals. However, there is a glimmer of hope - by reaching out, they have said that they want to change.

Let's consider a famous quote from Thomas Edison: "The definition of insanity is doing the same thing over and over again and expecting different results." If you genuinely desire change, you must embrace an approach you haven't tried before.

When it comes to a growth mindset, it is our job as coaches to expand your perspective on what is possible. Over time, we can demonstrate the theory we teach, and you will begin to achieve the results you seek. With a bit of self-awareness, you will be amazed at what is possible. Now that these mindsets have been brought to your attention, you'll start recognising fixed and growth mindsets everywhere.

I am fortunate to have a growth mindset and it's something that I have continually worked on. I am always trying to expand my horizons, believing that anything is possible if I put the work in. At the end of every weekly team meeting, I pose a question asking if we could do anything better or differently than we did last week to better serve our clients. This has resulted in several evolutions of the program, and currently we are on version 7 with the intention to revise it biannually.

Furthermore, I have engaged in numerous hours of one-on-one counselling, mentorship, business coaching and performance coaching. I understand and value an open mindset. By maintaining this open mindset and identifying a recurring problem within the gym industry, I've developed a program that delivers life-changing results for my clients.

With a growth mindset, I can primarily work from home. I enjoy breakfast with my family each day, walk the dogs on the moor each morning and spend precious time with my family throughout a normal working day. I can take time off whenever I want and have complete control over my destiny. With a growth mindset, I consistently maintain a certain level of health and fitness that allows me to perform at my best. With a growth mindset, I show my team and clients that life can be lived on your own terms. With a growth mindset, I decided to write this book. Writing isn't my strong suit, and I'm not particularly good at spelling. Writing this book challenged me in ways I didn't anticipate, but here we are, now there is a copy of the book in your hands. With a growth mindset, I overcame my stammer because I refused to let it control me. I can now speak publicly with confidence and ease because I believed I could learn that skill.

From this moment on, abandon any fixed mindset that you may have and actively seek solutions in everything you do. You will begin to see how to improve things at home, how to be more efficient and how to bring workplace improvements to your managers to showcase your value. You will also start to find ways to be a better parent, and you will become one.

Don't fall into the trap of always doing what you've always done. We can all be 1% better than we were last week. With small incremental changes, you can make huge transformations to all areas of your life.

Moreover, we've received feedback that our clients sometimes encounter negative responses about their progress from their peer groups. Often, these individuals are unaware of the impact of their comments and tend to have a fixed mindset. It's usually not their fault, they simply just lack the emotional awareness that our clients have now developed.

Negative comments from peer groups often stem from an insecurity within. They may be afraid, consciously or subconsciously, of losing their friend or partner, or of their friend or partner surpassing them. Such comments are typically meant to keep that person in their place. People resist change, which is why if you're aiming to change yourself – how you feel, or how you look for example. You need a supportive community of people who want the best for you and have the qualifications and life experience to guide you in the right direction.

Some of my clients have had friends who have called them too skinny, or said that they look unhealthy because they have dropped a few dress sizes when they could have healthily lost more weight. I've had a client whose partner deemed working out three times a week and hitting 5,000 steps a day obsessive when, in reality, it's just healthy. Peer groups can influence us positively or negatively, depending on their mentality.

Be warned: negativity may come your way when you start taking control of your health and fitness. But guess what? We're here every step of the way to support you through it if it arises.

20. You Don't Need Motivation, You Need Discipline

Whilst having been on the topic of mindset, I often hear prospective clients tell me that they just can't get motivated, and that's why they're reaching out. They feel stuck in a rut and unable to get started.

Relying solely on motivation to achieve your goals will never work. Motivation is a fickle beast. When times are good and you have plenty of available time, it's easy to feel motivated because there's nothing to worry about. Motivation to change is what prompts you to pick up the phone and call me. However, we quickly need to swap motivation for dedication. Dedication means acting without thinking too much, knowing that if you implement the plan, you'll reach your end goal. Becoming disciplined from the outset is crucial.

Let's consider an example:

You've had a terrible night's sleep and you wake up late for work. You rush out the door to avoid being late for your meeting, forget to take your lunch and you have no time for breakfast with the kids. When you get to work, you find out the meeting has been rescheduled. You chase your tail all day and end up finishing work late. Your gym session starts in 45 minutes, but even after a bad day, you show up and get it done, because you are disciplined. You know this phase or day will pass, and your gym session is a non-negotiable for you.

Can you see how relying on just motivation alone could lead you to skip your workout that day because you're not in the mood and want to unwind with a drink? Without discipline, this could easily become an ever-increasing pattern.

To take total control of your health and fitness, you need to become disciplined. Don't give yourself time to overthink or talk yourself out of anything. When you book your gym session, you are committing, and therefore it is your responsibility to make it happen, regardless of how bad your day has been.

As a quick side note on training days and times, you will naturally know what works best for you. Is it training in the early morning or late evening? You'll have a good idea based on your natural sleep and wake patterns. If you're more of a night owl, you'll probably prefer afternoon or evening workouts. If you're an early riser, morning workouts may be your preference to set yourself up for the day.

21. The Negative Reward Feedback Loop

This is something I want to bring to your attention: the tendency to justify indulging in something 'naughty' in response to struggle or conflict. An example of this would be reaching for a drink after a long, stressful day. It's seen as a reward for surviving the day, and a way to relax by taking control of something and then doing something that you know you shouldn't be doing.

Typically, this involves food, alcohol, or smoking. In most instances, it's treating yourself to something indulgent, often overconsuming food which is dense in calories, or alcohol. We all know the crisp sound of opening a beer or the pop of the cork from a bottle of your favourite wine, or perhaps the drag of a cigarette or vape.

We know categorically that these things are not good for us. In fact, we'd be far better off going for a power walk or heading to the gym for a workout, so why don't we? The simple answer is the time frame involved in a reward feedback loop. We are hardwired to crave instant gratification. We tend not to think too much about our future selves or how good it feels to be fit, strong and healthy, even though it's something we crave. In that moment, you want instant relief.

We need to understand that the fleeting feeling of happiness from doing something negative toward our health doesn't come anywhere close to the long-term satisfaction of feeling healthy, fit and strong. Yet, we find ourselves in a cycle of wanting to feel and possibly look better, but continually opting for the short-term satisfaction, over the long-term game.

We need to be acutely aware of these cycles and tendencies because it's behaviours and patterns like these that will hold you back from achieving your health and fitness goals. My advice is to break these cycles of behaviour as quickly as you can. Replace the 'bad' cycle with going out for a walk, going for a workout, or even eating an apple. Whatever your vice is, find a way to replace your negative behaviour with positive or neutral behaviours that only benefit you in the long run.

22. Understand What Is Possible, Then Make It Happen

We have seen many clients reach the top 5% of their population in terms of health, fitness and strength. They openly express that they look and feel the best they ever have in their lives, and they are content. Now, they simply want to focus on small incremental improvements to fine-tune, but in terms of their goals, they have surpassed their expectations and are satisfied with their progress with their health and fitness. This marks a significant success for us, indicating that we have effectively fulfilled our role, and our clients are healthy, happy and equipped with a plan to maintain their progress and continue improving incrementally.

We have also seen many other clients who achieve the top 5% of the population in terms of their health, fitness and strength, but they feel they have much more potential to tap into. This is always possible, and it is imperative that we expand their vision. It is our responsibility to clearly articulate and devise a precise roadmap for the client to follow to achieve their aspirations. Some clients may progress to the top 4%, top 3%, top 2%, or even the top 1% of the population, accomplishing feats they never deemed possible, such as running a marathon or completing their first triathlon.

Moreover, reaching the top 5% of the population instils intrinsic confidence into our clients, empowering them to deliver presentations at work or negotiate the pay raise they've postponed for months or even years. Achieving your health and fitness goals is highly individualised and unique to each person. We will support you as far as your body can physically go, or you can choose to maintain your progress whenever you feel you've reached peak physical and mental fitness.

Personally, I set my benchmark at being in the top 2% of the population at any given time throughout the year. I feel confident in my body and its capabilities. I believe that I devote enough time to myself while still managing my business, family and relationships effectively, and I feel I excel in my professional life, which holds significant importance for me.

For another client, their goal might be reaching a size 12, feeling confident at the beach and being a positive role model for their children, demonstrating how to balance motherhood while prioritising self-care. Everybody's goals are unique, but it's absolutely crucial to establish crystal-clear objectives that are achievable, healthy and sustainable.

In our program, we accompany you every step of the way, ensuring that you are fully aware of your progress and maintaining alignment with those principles.

23. Deciding on the End Goal

I have a life motto that I live by: "Dream so big it scares you". This sounds simple, right? Dream your dream, and then work your way back from there to make it happen. If you aren't excited or nervous about the thought or task at hand, you aren't thinking big enough. We are capable of more than we ever thought possible. As a coach, it is my job to paint your future for you and show you how far you can take your health and fitness. However, it is important to understand that we always need goals.

Think about anything you've ever achieved in your life. Perhaps it was buying your first house, obtaining a degree or getting your dream job – you strived to make it happen. Without goals, we lack direction, motivation and meaning in our lives. The same goes for your health and fitness.

So, when is enough, enough?

The answer should be: it will never be enough. I'm not talking about world domination, I'm talking about being slightly better than you were yesterday and striving to be the very best version of yourself. Personally, the thought of remaining stagnant in my health, fitness, strength, personal and professional life terrifies me. For me, standing still equals regression, thus undoing all the hard work I've put in to get to where I am today.

I actively embrace the chaos of positive change, and once you've created forward momentum, lean into that feeling and enjoy the ride. This is the philosophy I bring into my own life, and so should you. You are capable of much more than you ever thought possible. Don't allow life or circumstances to dictate your future or destiny. You can achieve anything you set your mind to; you just need to believe.

24. The Checklist

If you follow the 5 pillars, the program is simple. The adherence and consistency is key to success. To re-cap, the pillars are:

The Plan

- Your minimum exercise commitment per week - typically just 2-3 gym sessions per week
- Follow your nutritional plan
- Adhere to your hydration targets
- Honour your non-negotiables that must happen on a daily and weekly basis

The Training

- Strength training to ensure you get stronger every week
- Accessory training to ensure you are becoming functionally fit and strong
- Aerobic/Conditioning training for overall improvement of cardiovascular health

The Support

- No cap on the amount of support offered by the

coaching team

- Follow the prompts you receive each Sunday and Monday

The Accountability

- Your progress is constantly reviewed inline with your goals
- Your nutrition approach is also regularly reviewed
- Your workout frequency and intensity is regularly reviewed
- Critical, subjective feedback is the single most important factor when it comes to accountability

The Community

- You are surrounded by a group of like-minded, positive, friendly individuals

As you progress, we may need to tweak your plan slightly and coach around your lifestyle factors, such as family commitments, social engagements, careers, holidays, etc. but the template remains closely related across all of our clients.

Now that we have outlined the pathway to success in the program, it is crucial to ensure that you are moving up on the trajectory that has been set. It is vital that you are improving and progressing every quarter, and we must ensure that you are continually ascending through the levels. As a general rule, each percentage change in scoring (for example going from the top 5% to the top 4%) will typically take 6-12 months to achieve. For most clients, this is a 6+ year plan, which is more than enough to positively change your life forever.

25. Conclusion

Too many gyms have it wrong. Too often, you've been let down in the past. If you've joined a gym before, it's because you wanted results and there's a large chance that didn't happen for you. And if you're considering joining a gym, I urge you to do your research because the traditional gym model sets you up for failure.

As discussed, I am on a mission to revolutionise the outdated, traditional and ineffective membership model of gyms. I'm tearing down the walls of tradition and building a fitness revolution where everyone thrives and succeeds toward their goals, with an unstoppable community of like-minded individuals backing them every step of the way.

We know every single client by their first name, we know their goals and aspirations and we've hung out with them in social settings. Clients have made friendships for life and, more importantly, they have achieved results they never thought possible.

I hope by reading this book, you have a much greater understanding of why you need coaching and an incredible community backing you up to succeed on your health and fitness journey.

The Future Bodies' #GameChangers Program

The #GameChangers program isn't just another run-of-the-mill fitness plan – it's a three-week journey that will completely transform the way you approach health and fitness. Imagine stepping into a gym and immediately feeling the difference. That's what our kickstart program offers, a taste of the Future Bodies' experience that will leave you hooked from day one.

During these intensive three weeks, we'll arm you with everything you need to not just reach your goals but surpass them. It's not just about workouts and meal plans, it's about immersing yourself in a revolutionary approach to fitness that's shaking up the industry's outdated norms.

But here's the best part: this is just the beginning. After the kickstart, you'll have the option to continue your journey with us, where we'll be right by your side, cheering you on and guiding you toward continued success.

Are you ready to break free from the old, ineffective gym routines? Take the first step toward a healthier, fitter you by visiting our website, futurebodies.co.uk, and booking a consultation with one of the team.

Together, we'll map out a game plan tailored specifically to your needs and get you started on the journey of a lifetime.

Don't settle for being another statistic of the old gym model. Join us in the health and fitness revolution, where every member thrives, succeeds and transforms their lives with the support of an unstoppable community.

The Author

Josh Ware assumed the helm of Future Bodies in 2018 and introduced the groundbreaking #GameChangers program in 2021. With a steadfast commitment to transforming lives, he has crafted the #GameChangers program to wield a profound positive influence on every individual it touches. His mission? To impact thousands of lives through his innovative program.

Penning this book was a labour of love, born from his unwavering dedication. With a fervent passion for the subject matter, Josh believes passionately that the fitness industry must evolve.

Today, Josh remains intimately involved in the operations of his gym, with plans to open a second site in the near future. Alongside work, with his partner Jess, they are raising two small, incredible children, and two daft labradors!

Additionally, Josh is embracing opportunities in public speaking, having recently begun delivering talks at schools and events, where he's igniting the passion of the next generation of health and fitness coaches!

Special Thanks

I'd like to write a few special thank yous to people that have had an influence on my life and impacted me in more ways than they or I could have ever imagined.

Firstly, thank you to my parents for teaching me the lessons in life that have enabled me to get to where I am today.

I'd also like to say a huge thank you to my first boss and mentor, Andy. Andy, what you did for me and what you taught me quite literally revolutionised my approach to business and systems, and opened up my world of thinking bigger.

I would like to thank my incredible team, some of whom have been with me since the very beginning. Because of your steadfast dedication and belief, we have been able to create a truly unstoppable community and culture that is unrivalled in the fitness industry.

I'd also like to say a massive thank you to my clients for entrusting me with your health and fitness goals and allowing me to do what I love.

I would like to say a special thanks to the number of counsellors I have worked with over the years, your insights and clarity have helped me overcome many hurdles holding me back.

Additionally, I would like to mention a special organisation called the Starfish Project. Established in 1998, Starfish teaches techniques to help people who stammer gain control of their fluency and increase confidence. The training combines a breathing technique, avoidance reduction therapy and positive attitude development in a caring and supportive environment. Anne Blight, the founder, is the principal course coach and if anyone out there is struggling with their stammer I highly recommend reaching out to Anne and her team. They are a charity organisation and their approach to managing your stammer is second to none.

And, thank you to Jess. My partner in crime, my confidant and my companion on the journey of life and parenthood. Without you by my side and being an incredible mum to our children, I wouldn't be able to do what I do. You are the bedrock that holds our family unit together and for that I am forever grateful.

Yours, always, Josh.

And a final note to my beloved children.

As you embark on your journey through life, remember: the world is your oyster, and your dreams are the pearls waiting to be discovered. Never let anyone hinder your aspirations. Be bold, be extraordinary. Weigh every opportunity, trust your instincts, and follow the path you believe is right with unwavering courage. Your potential knows no bounds, so go forth, shine brightly, and illuminate the world with your brilliance.

With all my love and endless support Dad

x